Super
FUN
SCIENCE

with Cool and Challenging Experiments

BARRON'S

Contents

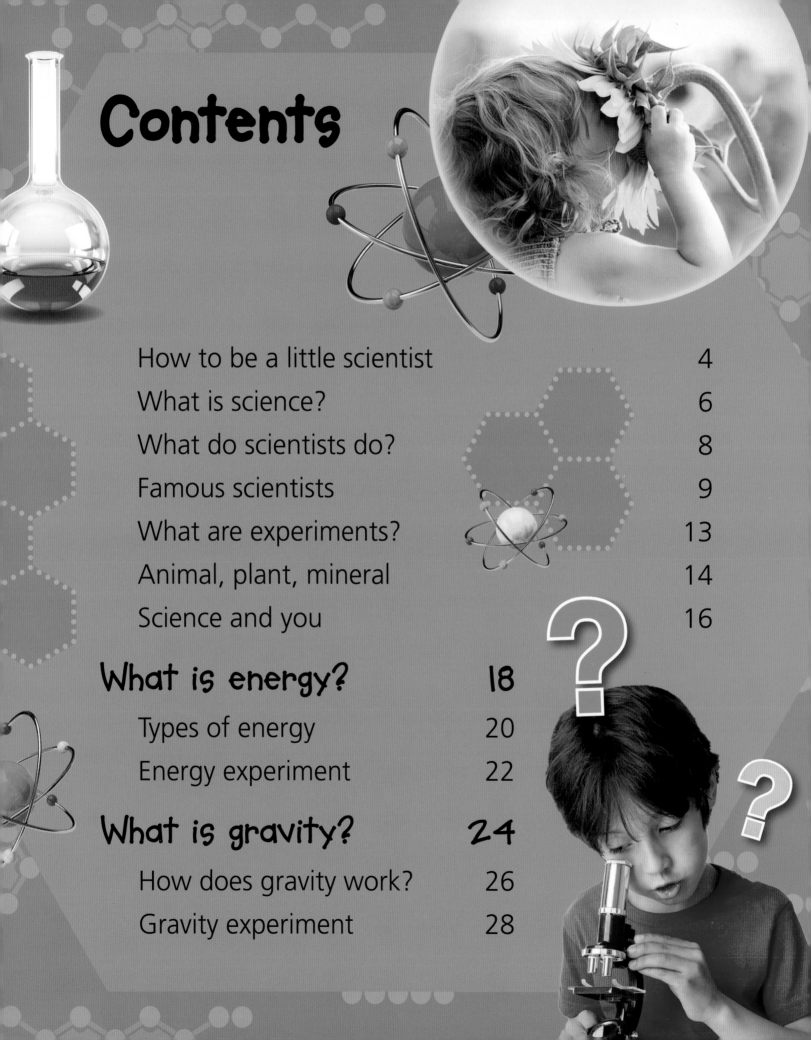

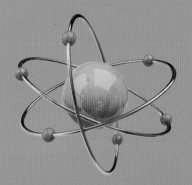

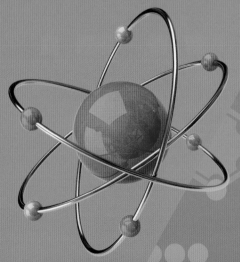

How to be a little scientist

Being a little scientist is all about exploring the world around you and figuring out how things work. It's about asking lots of questions and trying to find out the answers. Science is everywhere you look!

To become a real little scientist, you'll need some simple equipment. Most of these things can be found around your house.

Little scientist clothes

Safety goggles to protect your eyes from any splashes

Plastic gloves to keep your hands clean and to protect them

A cover-up to protect your clothes—a grown-up's old shirt will do

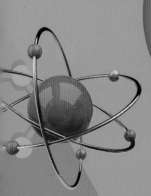

Little scientist tools

Magnifying glass
to help you look
closely at things

Tweezers
to pick up
small things

Flask or bottle
to hold big amounts
of liquids

**Test tubes or
little bottles**
to measure
small amounts
of liquids

Eyedropper
to add just a
few drops
at a time

Funnel
to make pouring
liquids easier

Safety first

Sometimes science
involves using and
mixing strange liquids.

**It's important to
always check with an
adult before you do
anything.**

To be safe, always follow these important rules:

🤚 **Always have a grown-up with you.**

🤚 **Always wear your cover-up, safety goggles,
and gloves.**

🤚 **Never touch food while doing experiments.**

🤚 **Get a grown-up to measure any liquids.**

🤚 **Wash your hands before and after experiments.**

🤚 **Always clean up when you have finished.**

What is science?

Now that you are a little scientist, you can try and figure out the why, how, what, and when of just about anything. Everything in our world happens for a reason, and science can show you what those reasons are.

Science explained

When grown-ups talk about science, they use lots of complicated words that describe the type of science they are interested in. There are seven areas of natural science, and they are all really interesting.

An easy explanation of these types of sciences is:

Astronomy—this is the study of outer space (that's everything way up past the sky). To make it easy for little scientists, we will rename this science *Star Gazing*.

Biology—this is the study of all living things. Let's call this *Nature Study*.

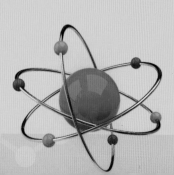

Chemistry—this is the study of everything you can touch, see, feel, or smell. This one requires lots of experiments, so let's call it *Hocus Pocus*.

Earth Science—this is the study of our planet Earth and what happens to it. It would be fun to call this *Our Mother Earth*.

Physics—this is the study of the world that we live in and how it works. This can be renamed *How Stuff Works*.

Atmospheric Science—this is the learning and understanding of our climate, weather, and water cycle. This can be called *Weather Works*.

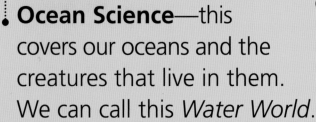

Ocean Science—this covers our oceans and the creatures that live in them. We can call this *Water World*.

What do scientists do?

Scientists are big thinkers. When scientists have ideas, they do experiments or tests to see if they are right or wrong. Science can be pretty surprising and sometimes the answers seem impossible.

Many scientists spend most of their time in laboratories (often called labs). A lab is a place that has all the equipment that is needed for a scientist to do his or her experiments.

Other scientists spend a lot of time outdoors, as that is where they need to be to do their work.

SUPER SCIENCE FACT

Scientists discovered that cats use their whiskers to check whether a space is too small for them to fit through.

Famous scientists

These famous scientists changed the way we understand our world with some very cool thinking. Perhaps one day you can be a famous scientist, too!

Albert Einstein

(1879–1955)

Albert Einstein thought about and tried to understand *How Stuff Works*. He wanted to know why and how everyday things happened.

Isaac Newton

(1643–1727)

Isaac Newton was interested in many of the natural sciences. He is probably best known for his work with gravity. He understood that gravity keeps our feet firmly on the ground and stops us from floating off into space.

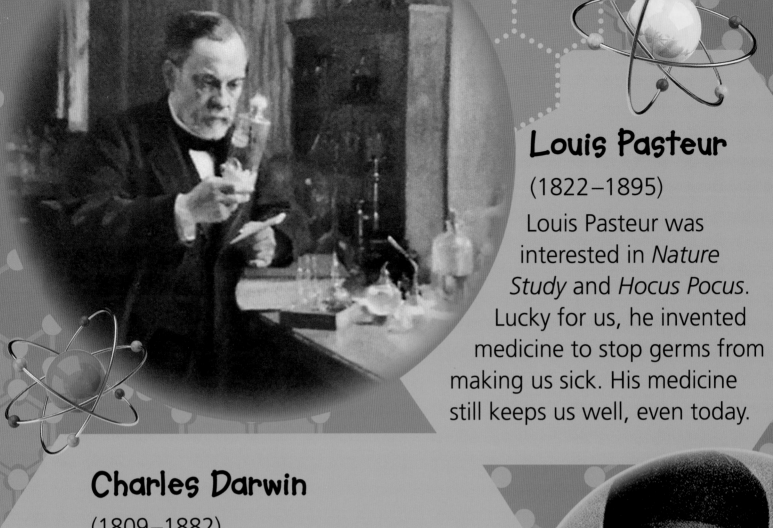

Louis Pasteur

(1822–1895)

Louis Pasteur was interested in *Nature Study* and *Hocus Pocus*. Lucky for us, he invented medicine to stop germs from making us sick. His medicine still keeps us well, even today.

Charles Darwin

(1809–1882)

Charles Darwin loved *Nature Study*. He sailed around the world filling books with beautiful drawings and descriptions of all the different animals and plants he saw.

SUPER SCIENCE FACT

Darwin was the first to try to convince people that animals and plants could "adapt" or change to fit in with their surroundings. In those days, people found this difficult to believe!

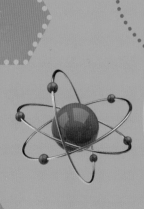

Galileo

(1564–1642)

Galileo was a true *Star Gazer* and is often called the first great scientist. He wasn't the first to invent the telescope, but he created one that could look even farther into the sky!

Marie Curie

(1867–1934)

Marie and her husband Pierre Curie worked in both fields of *How Stuff Works* and *Hocus Pocus*. They discovered and used something called radium to make X-rays. Every time you have an X-ray you can thank the Curies.

"Nothing in life is to be feared, it is only to be understood."

Edwin Hubble

(1889–1953)

Edwin Hubble was famous for *Star Gazing*. He discovered that there are galaxies beyond ours (the Milky Way). A special telescope was named after him called the Hubble Space Telescope.

Aristotle

(384 B.C.–322 B.C.)

Aristotle was a deep thinker whose science was *How Stuff Works*. Although he lived a long time ago, he developed many new and important scientific ideas that are still used today.

SUPER SCIENCE FACT

The light from stars takes millions of years to reach Earth, so looking at the night sky is like looking back in time!

What are experiments?

Experiments are ways for scientists (and little scientists) to test their ideas.

There are five main stages to all experiments:

1. Question
A question or problem that you don't know the answer to.

2. Think
Scientists need to think about what they believe will happen in the experiment.

3. Experiment
This can be done in a lab or outside.

4. Conclude
At the end of the experiment the scientist will have the answer or conclusion.

5. Do it again!
Repeating the experiment all over again will prove that the scientist has the true answer.

Ask questions

Animal, plant, mineral

Science tells us that nearly all natural things in the whole world are either animals, plants, or minerals!

So, the first thing little scientists can ask themselves about anything natural is: is it an animal, a plant, or a mineral? This helps us understand where things come from and what they are.

An **animal** is anything that is alive and breathes, eats, grows, and has babies.

A **mineral** is anything that isn't alive, doesn't grow, and comes from the ground.

A **plant** is also alive. It uses light from the sun to make its own food. Some plants also produce fruits and vegetables.

Animal, plant, mineral game

Little scientists love to think about things. So, let's look at some natural things and decide if each one is an animal, a plant, or a mineral! Use check marks to show what you think they are.

A fish

Animal

Plant

Mineral

You!

Animal

Plant

Mineral

Gold

Animal

Plant

Mineral

A tree

Animal

Plant

Mineral

An apple

Animal

Plant

Mineral

For answers to these questions, please turn to page 16.

Science and you

Science is all around us and affects us all, every day of the year from the moment we wake up, then all day long and right through the night.

Without science:

1. There would be no way to make or use electricity.

2. There would be no medicine to help us when we're sick.

Answers from page 15:
You (Animal)
A tree (Plant)
Gold (Mineral)
An apple (Plant)
A fish (Animal)

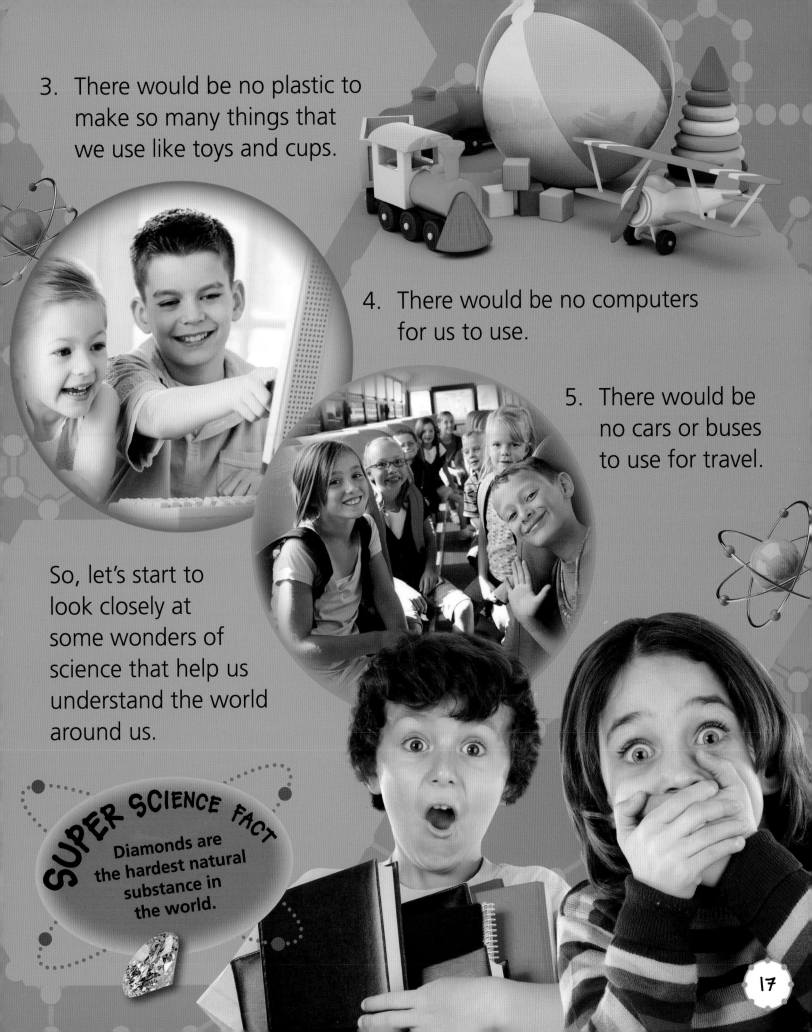

3. There would be no plastic to make so many things that we use like toys and cups.

4. There would be no computers for us to use.

5. There would be no cars or buses to use for travel.

So, let's start to look closely at some wonders of science that help us understand the world around us.

SUPER SCIENCE FACT

Diamonds are the hardest natural substance in the world.

What is energy?

Energy helps us do things. It gives us light. It warms our bodies and homes. It bakes cakes and keeps milk cold. It runs our TVs and our cars. It helps us grow, move, and think.

Energy is light

We need light so we can see. We get most of our light from the sun. At night, we must make our own light. Usually, we use electricity to make light.

Energy is heat

When we burn a piece of wood, we are using up the energy stored by the tree to make light and heat. This heat can then be used to cook food and warm our houses.

Energy makes things grow

All living things need energy to grow. Plants use light from the sun to grow. Animals, including people, eat plants and use the energy stored in them to grow.

Energy makes things move

It takes energy to make things move. Cars run on the energy in gasoline. Many toys run on the energy in batteries. Sailboats are pushed by the energy in the wind.

Energy runs machines

Electricity is energy and it runs our TVs and computers. We use electricity many times every day. It gives us light and heat, makes things move, and runs all the gizmos in our house.

Types of energy

We use the energy from electricity in many objects in our homes and cities. To provide us with all the electricity we need, scientists have invented ways of turning other types of energy into electricity.

Wind—we can get energy from wind.

Water—we can get energy from moving water.

Sunshine (Solar)—we can get energy from the sun.

Plants (Biomass)—we can get energy from plants and trees that get their energy from the sun.

Heat (Geothermal)—we can get energy from the heat in the Earth.

Nuclear—we can get energy from atoms (teeny tiny specks that make up things).

Coal/Oil/Gas—we get most of the energy we use from coal, oil, and gas.

SUPER SCIENCE FACT

The amount of energy in the world never changes, it stays exactly the same—energy can't be lost!

Energy experiment
Energy from the sun

What is a thermometer?

A thermometer tells us how hot or cold something is. The red or silver line in the middle of the thermometer moves up and down to show the temperature.

What you'll need

1. Three thermometers*
2. Sheet of black paper
3. Sheet of white paper
4. Sunshine!

*If you don't already have three thermometers, you can ask a grown-up to help you make them. Use the Internet to find instructions.

Energy question

Do some colors soak up more heat from the sun than others?

Step 1

Put the three thermometers in a sunny place.

Step 2

Cover the bulb of one thermometer with black paper. Cover the bulb of one thermometer with white paper. Leave the remaining thermometer uncovered.

Step 3

Write down which of the three thermometers you think will get the hottest.

Step 4

Wait a few minutes. Check the thermometers and write down how hot they got. Were you right?

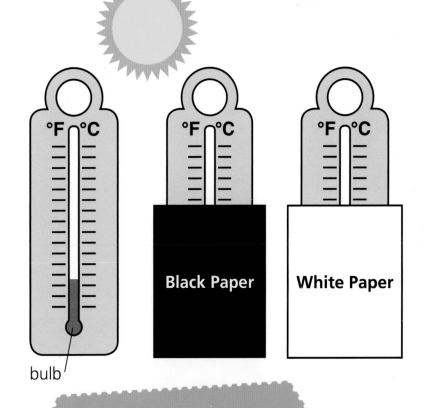

bulb

Black Paper

White Paper

LITTLE SCIENTIST HINT:
The higher the temperature, the longer the red or silver line.

What is gravity?

Gravity has been around forever. Gravity is the invisible force that keeps us and the air around us from floating away. It's very useful.

Gravity is what keeps you on the ground and what causes things to fall to the ground when we drop them. Where would we be without gravity?

Gravity and planets

Gravity is what makes planets like Earth move around the sun. Gravity is what makes the stars clump together in huge, swirling galaxies. Outer space would be very different without gravity!

Gravity and tides

This might come as a surprise, but it's gravity from the sun and the moon that makes the ocean's tide rise and fall.

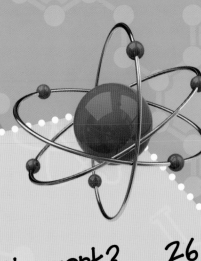

How does gravity work?

Gravity works on everything in the world. You cannot see how gravity works, but it is always working.

Gravity works on plants, animals, and people. It works on water, metal, and wood—on absolutely everything! Astronauts know that when they are out in space, they cannot feel Earth's gravity. That is why everything floats in space, even water.

SUPER SCIENCE FACT

An apple falling on Isaac Newton's head is what made him begin to think about gravity. Ouch, that's a hard way to learn a lesson!

Gravity holds things down . . . everything on Earth. I bet you thought it pushes you to the ground. Wrong! Gravity never pushes.

Gravity always pulls. It pulls everything toward the center of Earth. It holds the water in the sea, the cars on the road, and you on the ground. Gravity tells us which way is up and which way is down. When you run and trip, you always fall down, not up. That is gravity working.

Gravity experiment
Hit the ground

What you'll need

1. A shoe

2. A piece of paper scrunched into a ball

Gravity question

Which object will hit the ground first: the shoe or the scrunched paper?

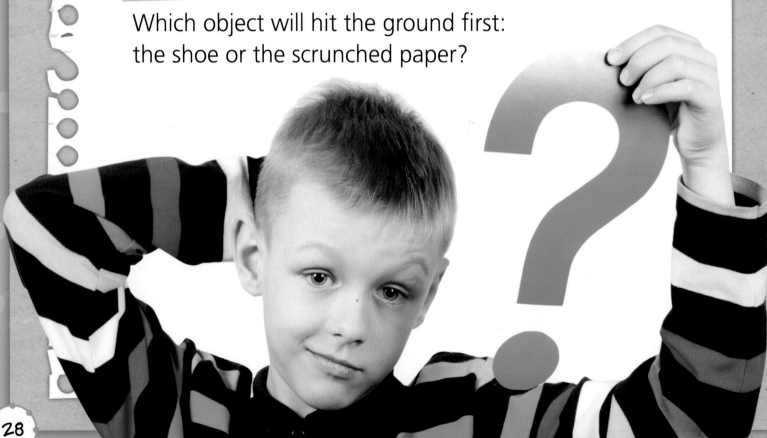

👋 Step 1

Write down which object you think will hit the ground first.

👋 Step 2

Hold the shoe in one hand and the paper ball in the other.

👋 Step 3

Hold both objects high in front of you at equal heights.

👋 Step 4

Release both objects at the same time.

👋 Step 5

Write down which object hit the ground first. Were you right? To be a *careful* little scientist, repeat this experiment a few times to check that the answer is always the same.

What is weight?

Weight and gravity are connected. Weight is what you get when gravity pulls on something.

So, something might weigh a lot here on Earth because the gravity pull is strong, and float in the air on the moon where the gravity pull is less strong.

Weight and mass

Weight and mass are different. Mass is the amount of **stuff** in an object. An object's mass always remains the same, unless part of it is taken away.

Neptune

Uranus

Saturn

Jupiter

Mars

Sun

Earth

Venus

Mercury

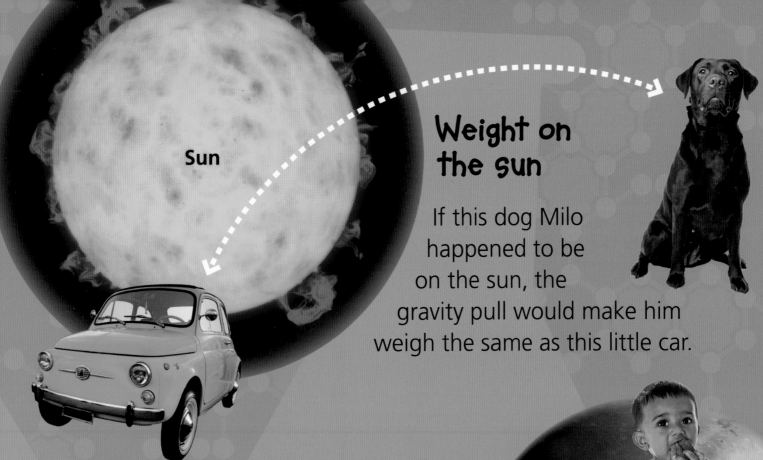

Sun

Weight on the sun

If this dog Milo happened to be on the sun, the gravity pull would make him weigh the same as this little car.

Weight on Mars

If this cute goat just happened to be on Mars, the gravity pull would make him as light as this little baby.

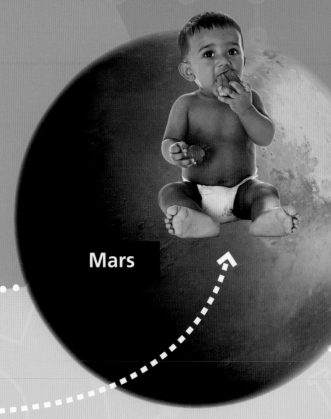

Mars

Earth

How does weight work?

We can easily measure the weight of most things on Earth, but we need scientists to tell us how much things would weigh on other planets.

How to measure weight

Here on Earth, there are different things we can use to measure weight. When cooking, we use a kitchen scale. To measure how much people weigh, we use a bathroom scale. For really big things, like trucks, we need special truck weigh stations.

How much do you weigh in outer space?

Have you ever wondered how much you would weigh in outer space? Well, it would depend on what planet you were standing on.

Your mission is to figure out what your weight would be as you jump from one planet to another.

Because you don't have your own spaceship to take you to the planets, we have made it easier for you by giving you the gravity pull on each planet. So, grab a calculator and ask a grown-up to help you figure this out.

My Earth weight = _____ pounds

PLANET	GRAVITY PULL	Multiply the gravity pull by your Earth weight to get your "space" weight
Mercury	0.4	
Venus	0.9	
Earth (your home)	1	
Mars	0.4	
Jupiter	2.5	
Saturn	0.9	
Uranus	0.8	
Neptune	1.2	

SUPER SCIENCE FACT

An elephant weighs the same as 50 men, but if it were standing on the sun, the elephant would now weigh the same as 1,400 men!

Wherever you are in the solar system, your mass will stay exactly the same. You will always look like you even though you will weigh more or less—that's gravity for you!

Weight experiment
Making scales

These scales can be made with bits and pieces that you find around the house. Once you complete this experiment, you will have everything you need to weigh most things.

What you'll need

1. Small cardboard box
2. Paper clips
3. String
4. Push pin
5. Ruler

6. Rubber band
7. Lined paper and a black felt-tip pen
8. Piece of poster board
9. Tape

✋ Step 1

Ask a grown-up to press the push pin into the top of a long, narrow piece of poster board. Tape a piece of lined paper to the poster board. This will be your scale card.

✋ Step 2

Loop a rubber band inside the paper clip, and then hang the paper clip from the push pin. Ask a grown-up to help you.

✋ Step 3

Throw away the lid of the cardboard box. Ask a grown-up to make one hole in each corner near the top edge of the box. Tie a piece of string to each corner of the box, and use tape to hold it in place if necessary.

✋ Step 4

Tie the ends of the pieces of string together, and then tie them to the end of the rubber band. It now looks like a hot air balloon without the balloon.

✋ Step 5

On the scale card, use the pen to mark the point at the bottom end of the rubber band before you weigh an object. Mark how far down this point comes when you have something in the box. Use a ruler to measure the distance.

✋ Step 6

Weigh lots of different things and see what the heaviest object you can find is.

Can you guess which is heavier?
A plastic cup or a ceramic cup?
An apple or a banana?
A plastic block or
a wooden building block?

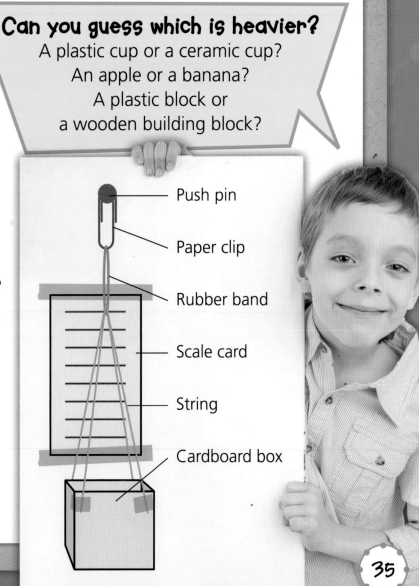

Push pin

Paper clip

Rubber band

Scale card

String

Cardboard box

35

What is light?

Light is everywhere in our world. We need it to see. Most of the light we get on Earth comes from the sun, but we also get light from lightbulbs.

What is light made of?

Light is made up of billions of small particles called photons (say *fo-tons*), which move in waves. The sun shines white light to Earth, but it doesn't look that way. The white light is made up of the seven colors of the rainbow. The blue part of the sun's light is what makes our sky look blue.

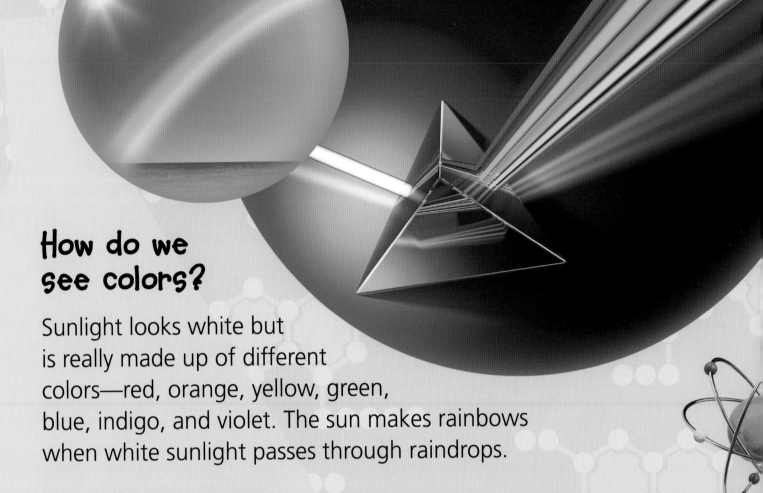

How do we see colors?

Sunlight looks white but is really made up of different colors—red, orange, yellow, green, blue, indigo, and violet. The sun makes rainbows when white sunlight passes through raindrops.

How fast is light?

Light travels in a straight path and moves very fast. In one second, light can go around Earth seven and a half times!

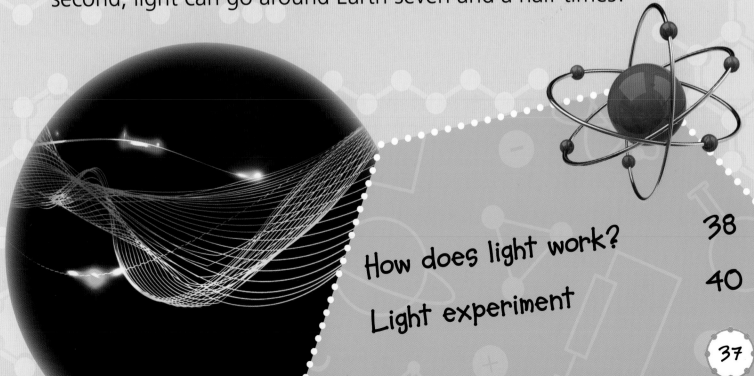

How does light work?

Light works in three main ways. I bet you didn't know that it can reflect, bend, and spread!

How light reflects

Light waves will reflect or bounce off things like a mirror. The only reason we can see the things around us is that light—either from the sun or from something like an electric lightbulb here on Earth—reflects off of them and into our eyes.

SUPER SCIENCE FACT

Sunlight can reach a depth of up to 262 feet (80 meters) in the ocean!

How light bends

Light waves can bend or change direction. This happens when light shines on water, glass, or plastic. When light waves bend, they slow down. When you see a mirage that looks wavy, it is a result of the light waves being bent by the hot air or by water.

How light spreads

Light waves bend and spread when there is something in their way. This is why when you sit in front of a light, the shadow behind you is bigger than you are.

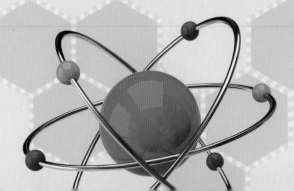

Light experiment
Bending light

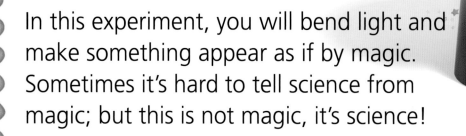

In this experiment, you will bend light and make something appear as if by magic. Sometimes it's hard to tell science from magic; but this is not magic, it's science!

What you'll need

1. A coin
2. A glass of water
3. Enough glue gel to stick under the coin
4. A bowl made out of something that you can't see through

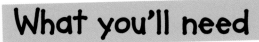 Step 1

Place the glue gel in the middle of the coin.

Step 2

Press the coin in the center of your bowl so that it will not move when you pour water into the bowl.

🖐 Step 3

Move backward away from the bowl until you cannot see the coin on the bottom of the bowl.

🖐 Step 4

Very slowly pour some water into the bowl until the coin starts to appear before your eyes. **How is this happening?** You haven't moved and you know that the coin is stuck to the bottom.

🖐 Step 5

Pour a bit more water into the bowl, and continue watching as more of the coin appears.

What you are seeing is an illusion made by light bending. This feels like magic, but it's not. It could be why some magicians are called *illusionists*—they are using science to trick you!

What is matter?

Matter is all the **stuff** around you. Everything on Earth is made up of matter.

How big is matter?

Matter can be big and it can be small. Chocolate cake is made up of matter. You are made of matter. The trees in your yard are made of matter. The furniture in your house is made of matter. Everything is made of matter!

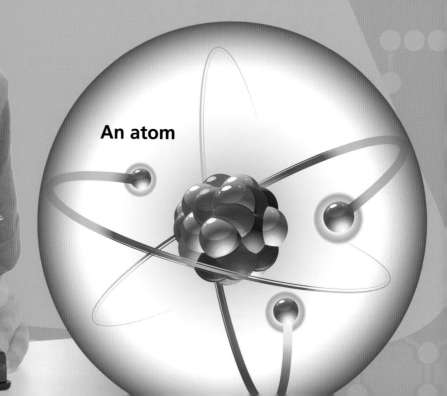

An atom

Atoms

All matter is made up of tiny building blocks called *atoms*. Atoms are so small that you can't see them without a really special, ultra-powerful microscope.

If you have two or more atoms stuck together, then you have a molecule (say *moll-uh-cyool*).

What is matter made of?

Matter comes in three main forms that are all made up of these tiny atoms:

1. **Solid**
2. **Liquid**
3. **Gas**

Solid matter

Solid matter is anything that has a size and a shape. The only way solids can change their shape is by force.

For example, if you bite an apple with your teeth or chop a block of wood with an axe you have changed their shape.

In solid matter, the atoms are tightly packed together and locked into place.

SUPER SCIENCE FACT

An atom is mostly made up of empty space. The chair that you're sitting on, this apple, even your own body, is mostly empty space. Amazing but true!

Liquid matter

Liquid must be kept in a cup or bottle for it to have a shape. Milk, water, and juice are all liquids.

The little atoms in liquids are not as close together as in solids, and they bounce around and pass each other easily.

Gas matter

Gas matter is hard to see because it has no shape. If you take a deep breath and blow into a balloon, your balloon fills up with air, and air is made up of many gases.

The little atoms in the air move quickly into the balloon. There is a lot of free space in between them, so they crash into the side of the balloon, making the balloon grow bigger.

Changing matter

A really cool thing about matter is that it can change. For example, water is a liquid. You can pour it into a glass. But, if you put it in the freezer for a while it becomes a solid ice cube. And, presto! It changes from liquid to solid.

Matter experiment
Let's trap gas

In this experiment, you will see what gases can do when they are caught in something.

Matter question

If gas is invisible, how do we know it's there?

What you'll need

1. A bottle of soda
2. A balloon
3. A watch

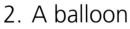

Step 1

Open the bottle of soda and carefully set it on a table.

Step 2

Quickly slip the end of the balloon over the neck of the bottle.

Pull the balloon's end down over the bottle top so that it fits tightly.

Step 3

Check on the balloon every 10 minutes for any changes. Has it changed shape?

What happened?

Soda is carbonated (say *car-bon-ated*). This means that it has air bubbles.

When you open the bottle, you hear a fizzing sound, and the gas can now escape out of the water, making bubbles.

As the gas has nowhere else to go but into the balloon, it makes the balloon blow up. Now we can see gas as it fills the balloon!

Science questions for you

Here are some science questions for you to figure out.

Happy research!

- Why is the sky blue?
- What is a rainbow?
- What is electricity?
- Where does electricity come from?
- How do seeds grow?
- Why do leaves fall off trees in autumn?
- How do cars work?
- Why does ice float in my drink?
- What are germs?
- How do airplanes fly?
- What's inside Earth?